There's a Brevitist Loose in the Condensory

—————————— *or* ——————————

If You Want Your Heart Broken, Read Somebody Else

EPIGRAMMATIC POETRY BY

John T. Langfeld

THERE'S A BREVITIST LOOSE IN THE CONDENSORY
OR
IF YOU WANT YOUR HEART BROKEN,
READ SOMEBODY ELSE

iUniverse books may be ordered through booksellers or by contacting:

iUniverse
1663 Liberty Drive
Bloomington, IN 47403
www.iuniverse.com
1-800-Authors (1-800-288-4677)

ISBN: 978-1-4917-2278-7 (sc)
ISBN: 978-1-4917-2277-0 (e)

Library of Congress Control Number: 2014903426

Printed in the United States of America.

iUniverse rev. date: 03/19/2014

Contents

Acknowledgments

Previously Published Poetry

"Annulment" (retitled here as "The Eye Didn't See It")
in *Of Summer's Passing*, National Library of Poetry, 1998

"Arrested Myth"
in *Curbside Splendor E-Zine*, October 2013

"The Last Laugh"
in *Curbside Splendor E-Zine*, October 2013

All photography by John T. Langfeld

Introduction

It is clear to me that my teaching and writing voices are similar. Although my teaching voice is long-winded while my writing voice is not, I am always attracted to language that titillates, cajoles, angers, and pokes fun—not always in that order. Apparently, that is truer on paper than it is in the air.

As a writer, I am a minimalist. Most everything I pen is short, exploring perceptual shifts that may or may not be obvious, that may or may not be spiked with humor. There is no rule that delimits poetry from exploring relevance with humor. Funny bones can be serious business. They can be perfect foils to keep us from missing points.

Recently my work has been called "epigrammatic," a term joined at the hip with adjectives like "aphoristic" and "apothegmatic." I prefer the moniker "brevitist." It is easier on the tongue.

Over time, this devotion to brevity has become essential to the ongoing struggle of keeping self-indulgence at bay. That process began when I realized that …

> God rested two days
> and never told anybody.

Part 1

Articulating the Madness

The Voyeur

The endless search
does 'round about about
set nigh upon the head
that wanders wanders
there (and here)
      a prize,
      a book,
      a look.

The endless search
does 'round about about
set nigh upon what's read
and pondered pondered
here (and there)
a voyeur's prize:
      a look,
      a glance,
      a chance-connection made
      or sold
      or bought.

The endless search
does 'round about about
set nigh upon what's said
or read
or seen
or grasped in furtive glee
a voyeur's prize,
       the endless search itself itself:
       a look,
       a book,
       an image made or laid
       or bought
       or sold
or simply followed followed,
here and there and there (and there),
           an endless search itself itself,
           a voyeur's prize.

Arrested Myth

God rested two days
and never told anybody.

Art Snarls

Philosophical territorialism flinches
when direct, unpolemic art
opens its mouth to lay referentials bare.

"Philistines!" art snarls,
with eyes wide in disbelief
at the backside of art's hasty exit.

Articulating the Madness

Cryptic is as cryptic does,
silly labels articulating the madness
(sadness)
of encrypted specificity.

Boxes of Soap

It is an incredible thing to be held
accountable for things over which
you have no control.

It is an incredible thing to realize that
credibility's so fragile,
and yet,
and yet
it is this fragility that keeps us human,
that keeps us from cloning a species devoid
of closets
and mirrors
and boxes of soap.

Merry Christmas

The reason for the season wears and tears the weary souls who
reason that the season soon will pass among the proles who
neither see nor hear nor understand, who
ornament unkind pretense, who
color ev'ry whisper, ev'ry cry, and ev'ry cheer to obfuscate who
does not get it, will not get it, will not let it be.

What means this rhyme, this verse that's terse, the reason for this folly?
You say you want what's writ to be more clear, a tad more jolly?

Bah, etc.

Disco Guilt

She sings of guilt
as if a rhythmic snap of the finger
purges it from the soul.

It's a hard tune to learn, and
it may not tell the whole tale.

Drafting

Drafting makes our flight less work, but
look what you follow
and rethink the journey.

Peon

Where do you *think*
the word "peon" came from?

Enjoying Sin Comes Later

They told us the age of reason was seven.
They said we knew what sin was then.

Hell,

enjoying sin came later.

Damn nuns.

Fate's Cold Hand

One never knows
when Fate's cold hand
will slap Reality's face.

Odd punishment.

Gag

Truly,
the sun must gag on occasion
at the progeny of its warmth.

Relevance

Depends it all
how you look at it
on.

Fear and Loathing, Part 1

It is not kosher
to pickle so my dreaming
in jars of reason.

Fear and Loathing, Part 2

This is fear talking: *run!*
This is courage talking: well, maybe tomorrow.

Pray, Tell Me

To sigh a prayer to garner some unjust reward
is labeled "fraud" by those whose ways are set
to fly above the fray that binds
the mind, the heart, the soul
to hallowed words
of fear.

Prophecy

People are not faithless,
only unfaithful
to the promise
of their own prophecy.

Sisyphus

The Myth of Sisyphus did fuss
and fuss and fuss and fuss and fuss
until such time as mem'ry's truss
forgot the rolling stone to trust
the telling of the tale to us
who roll the rock and roll the rock
and fuss and fuss and fuss and fuss.

This Dilemma Has Horns

The only thing more difficult
than being brilliant and not admitting it
is being brilliant and admitting it.

Surely You Jest

Shirley asked Judy
why she was attracted to men
who were smart
and talented
and strange.

Good question.

Easy answer:
      Judy is smart
      and talented
      and strange.

Hard answer:
      It's safe,
      and it punishes her.

Sylvia

who swallowed whole her gift,
spitting up parts upon parchment
meant for people she truly despised, yet
wanting forgiveness
for the wrath she made herself into,

who sought life's tomb,
calling it tardy,
lacking the guts to seek it on time,

who was reticent to anger,
too slowly amused
by life's sour taste
and the waste of it,

who bedded a man with good books
(not looks)
and sent him the bill
for the hemorrhage of her selfishness,

whose words were a shotgun emission
toward a world too distant a target.

Texting Adam

What I am thankful for:
    bees,
    pomegranates,
    language,
    ink.

What I am not thankful for:
    sterility,
    decay,
    illiteracy,
    cell phones.

    Cell phones?

Sure.

Imagine Eve texting Adam.

The Dissonance Trick

Dissonance,
you are so naturally beautiful,
like fire,
like rain,
like breathing in and out.

Consonance,
you create the lie
that makes you so appealing,
pimp for the dissonance trick.

The Eye Didn't See It

The difference between married and marred:
the drop of an "I."

The First Clue

The worst penance?
When there's no one to confess to.

The Gay Critic

Above Monet, below Judy Garland:
now, *that's* stature.

Empty Glasses

The mirror exists because of good backing,
though the glass gets all the credit.

Can Ye Not Spell Salieri?

To know one's gift is eclipsed
though the fame remains
is a stranger hell
than to be helpless, condemned
in excellence.

To know this hell,
look through the eyes
of the second-rate
who are told they are first
but know better.

Working Hard to Make Rain Pretty

This was easy:
>Rain beats at my window
>like the ultimate drum cadence,
>rhythm neither dictated by man
>nor inhibited by the arrogance
>of his choices
>or design.

>The cadence of water on glass is not ominous,
>like those heavenly hooves written of before,
>but the free, indeterminate music
>we so often ignore and label
>as unnatural.

This was hard:
>Rat-a-tat-tat
>is really all that
>we can make of clouds leaking water.

>Imagine at that
>it is all old hat,
>and forget the will to feel hauteur.

Fleecing Mary

The roses weren't red,
the lilacs were dead, and
the cow ran into the moon.

The pie had no plum,
Jack pushed his Jill, and
the three blind mice weren't really.

Humpty jumped,
the prince lost his shoes, and
the princess ate her pea.

Mary had a fish,
Rapunzel had a buzz cut, and
Little Red found the wrong house.

Juliet's black,
Robin kept the loot, and
the three musketeers were lovers.

Your mother lied.

Bravado

The mice will show off
in the absence of a cat.

The Mad Hatter Was Alice

She came into the room as Alice with malice
and pissed on the White Rabbit.

She walked off the page
and closed the book.

The end.

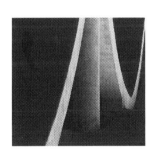

Part 2

The Brevitist in
the Condensory

A Pen in the Forest

What do you do when a writer's pen scratches
those nagging itches of dissatisfaction
with prism-sentences that loathe color and then yell,
"Timbre!"?

You listen for the noise.

Humility

The best kind of humility:
to know just how great you are.

Living within Without

Integrity …
one of those things
you live within
or die without knowing
you were dead within
without it.

Holy Cow

Toilet-paper the moon
and wipe the sky clean
of earth's excrement,
then watch the cow freak.

Righteous Indignation

So what if I can't spell.
Fuck of!

Keep the Change

Talking to people who won't change is like driving through your old neighborhood.

Clever Sun, Clever Moon

I

The sun is very clever.
It makes us think the moon is pretty
when really
it is ugly,
barren
like a dead person.

II

The moon:
the ultimate ventriloquist.

Beware of Pretty Things

Winged creatures soared between the high-rise buildings by the lake, wings translucent gold in the bright light of morning.

Wait.

Some asshole left the morning paper on his balcony for the wind to eat. Pretty is as pretty does and not as pretty seems.

An Old, Old Soul

Her words were (as usual)
an unusual mix
of birds,
of angels,
of bloodred pictures of silence
screaming to get out alive; yet
she has looked happiness in the face
and survived the disappointment.

"Life is not so much difficult as time-consuming," she said.

How like her.

The Unfolding

What you see is not what you get.
You get what you see,
which may be, as yet,
unfolding.

So look on, but beware.

What you see
may only be some haughty reflection
of its own viewing,
which may be, as yet,
unfolding.

Empty Rhetoric

Exorcise this exercise in blank verse or not,
or become flabbergasted by paucity's practice.

>   *Paucity's practice?*

Yes.
Otherwise, empty rhetoric wouldn't have a name.

>   *Empty rhetoric has a name?*

Yes.
It has several.

Blah, Blah, Blah, Blah, Blah.

Admit It ...

Evolution,
the ultimate example
of "pay it forward."

A Bromide for Life's Teeth

It is better to be an adjective
than it is to be a verb.

Verbs get all the attention.
Adjectives do all the work.

Editor Heaven

Be still, my darlings.
There is life after erasure.

The Last Laugh

When death comes,
the long and short of it is
the act has no curtain, no bow,
and no empty seats.

Gimme My Meds

There's a new disorder in town: manic expressive (ME).
It could be worse; they could change the moniker: NME.

Logic and Art

If waiting for Wagner to make his point
makes you want to reach for a joint,

if waiting for Schubert to finish a phrase
makes you not want to hold out for days,

don't think that Beethoven's grip on your throat
is some kind of quality effort.

The Conjugation

Evil has never been mandatory
but raises its hand to be called on,
to be, as in:

> *is are was were be been have*
> *had shall will should could might*
> *do did done.*

Sister taught us that.

She was mandatory.

Psalm 151

¹Oh god of science, how long must we wait for your grace;
        how long must we follow false promise and fear?
²Oh god of science, how shall we miss what you've given
        to guide and direct us to righteousness, cheer?

³Zealots cry, "Foul," and with reckless ambition
        raise flags and fake crosses, forgetting your name.
⁴They lie, cheat, and steal to bury your spirit,
        your goodness replaced by unwarranted blame.

⁵Oh god of science, how long must we bear false witness;
        how long before righteousness takes its place?
⁶Yet we sing and we praise your goodness
        and are mute to the zealots ignoring your grace.

Psalm 152

[1]Remember me, oh Lord, as one who backbiteth and taketh up reproach with reason.

[2]Play ye not the king of the hill, the keeper of sanctuary, the arbiter of treason.

[3]Love me as I love thee, with forgiveness and hope.

The Trick

Part of the trouble is Ms. Faulkner's odd, distracted manner. No.
Part of the trouble is *with* Ms. Faulkner's odd, distracted manner.

On the one hand, she *is* odd and distracts easily.
On the other hand, her behavior merely disguises the fact
that she spends most of her time on her knees,
never getting paid for servicing her clients.

From time to time, however, Sister sits down.

Solve for X

f times x *over* g times x (the whole unit, prime) *equals*
f-prime times g times x *minus*
f times x times g-prime times x *over*
g times x (the whole unit squared)

All this reads like a manual for sex.
I still don't know what to do with my tongue.

A Line in the Sand

Cause and effect are randomly formed.

If you think it's not so, go for Baroque,
but riding *that* horse keeps Descartes out in front,
not behind.

Unrandomly

Randomly formed, she sat,
hoping and hoping she'd clearly be all
she was up to be cracked; don't you see?

She was randomly formed,
warming and warming to the fact, the idea that
she may on her luck be not down on her knees
with those slight-of-hand tricks not standing.

Randomly formed she spat with her teacher
who tried so to reach her with chapters and verses.
She clearly rehearses, referently boggling intrusion and folly,
confusing, abusing, and using the time.

"I am BIC, pent up meter," she said randomunly.
"Adhere to my feet or be ready to stumble or mumble
or tweet as you fit see." She's ready for splaying
at hide-and-go-seek and the find ye shall plunder asunder;
no wonder she lost both the train and the dress of her thought.

Randomly formed, she sat.

Courage Is a Subtle Bitch

Courage is not always dramatic, heroic,
something you see on the ten o'clock news.

Sometimes she calls from a visual encounter,
like a wheelchair in the middle of a busy street,
like a body looks when the memory's gone,
like a Down syndrome baby, all smiling and shit,
like a casket where once there was humor and love,
like a push that's a shove with no bootstraps.

The Penultimate Snub

Somewhere so over the rainbow
Judy and Whitney and Janis and Amy
refused to move the "s" in their exits
to its rightful place.

Implications

They call me Higgs Boson.
They think I am God.

They call 'em as they see 'em.
They can't help themselves.

They won't believe in me long.
They never do.

Stickerbumped

I am just as good
as they say I'm not.

Francophilean Invective

The French all sing the same song:
"I love parrots …"

Ye Cannot Break a Heart with Mirth

Irk may never pleasant, ever-present be,
but smirk ye not this murk of language
put in place to lurk behind the cirque
of grand encounter—tedious work.

It may thus seem like too much rhyme
to season ev'ry verse with idle clatter; surely
no one wants to hear, within the kirk of verbal patter,
this:

"Yea noise? Then I'll be brief. O happy dirk!"

Vogue

hash opium cannabis speed
downers acid mushrooms weed

leaves seeds blotters pills
munchies red-eye busses chills

hotels backrooms toilets cars
bedrooms tearooms brothels bars

needles joints camels glass
toking poking using ass

move on

If a Digit Falls in the Forest

If goatskin or sheepskin or lambskin were used
for taking on pigment from quills or a press,

and cellulose, vellum, and pulp were recused
from bettering the fettering and wisering the guess,

this poem might look pretty for some time to come,
all squiggles and curls, all in love with itself,

but it's likely to crumble and finally succumb
like the rest of us fading up there on the shelf.

Get a grip.

Digits make noise.

Misappropriation

What did the waistline say to the belt?
Don't let the asbestos.

Spell Check Hell

He who spells opts, stop, and post just fine one day
but tops that with rampant misspelling the next
probably can't spell hits.

Facebook

You can easily click *like,* but
you have to spell *phhtthh.*

In Effable Means

When the cat's got them tongues,
it don't mean they cain't still wag,
but it sure as shootin' makes it hard fer them
to wrap theirselves around a thing or two
like that sissy feller pushin' stupid rocks.

You Know Who and What You Are

Writers call you many things:
pale medallion, neon scythe,
monstrous crystal, worn shell,
sing-along dot, mistress, thief,
all for color's sake, or Pete's.

They don't know.

Sometimes, moon is just a verb.

Found in the Shuffle

If political Al and writer Gert each had the other's last name, imagine what she would be called once they married.

Astrology's Backside

You want me to introduce myself?

My sun forms a square pattern with Uranus.

My sun and my Jupiter each harmoniously aspect Saturn.

My sun is conjoined with Jupiter and Mercury.
My Venus is conjoined with Mars and Neptune.
My Mars is conjoined with Neptune.

My moon is in an inharmonious aspect with Mercury.
My Mercury and my Jupiter are each in an inharmonious pattern with Uranus.

In the tropical zodiac, my sun is in Virgo; my moon, in Pisces.
In sidereal zodiac, my sun is in Leo; my moon, in Aquarius.

My sidereal sun is in the decanate of Sagittarius, which is ruled by Jupiter.
My sidereal moon is in the decanate of Libra, which is ruled by Venus.

You want me to be more direct?
Let's see …

My sun has designs on Uranus.

My sun and my Jupiter fuck around with Saturn.
My sun fucks Jupiter, but also Mercury.

Mars and Neptune both fuck Venus,
but Mars does Neptune on the side.

Mercury is not so into my moon,
like he and Jupiter aren't into Uranus.

My sun and my moon screw Virgo and Pisces,
doing Leo and Aquarius on the side.

My sun likes three-ways with Jupiter and his slut, Sagittarius,
my moon, with Libra and her pimp, Venus.

Apparently, Uranus is safe.

Polémica

Like the commissural fornicis,
that triangular subcallosal plate of commissural fibers
that curve back in the contralateral fornix,
words have no feelings.

Really?

Fuck you.

A Poem Speaks

I am short.

Read between the lines.
Look up the big words.

Make room for the silence that needs to sing
in the reading, in the heeding
of things you may not understand.

Google me where I am ticklish.

Sagrada Familia, Barcelona, Spain (Antoni Gaudi)
Photograph by John T. Langfeld, 2005

The Kiss

In the warmth of the corner of the outside wall
two men kissing, locked in the act,
Judas in a flowing robe
raising his left arm like a girl might,
placing her hand gently behind her man's neck,
ready for the blush of love's first kiss.

The Mentor

There he is,
the man who laid my feelings
bare
like scorched earth.

"Call me teacher," he said.
"Maybe tomorrow," I said.

He was fully clothed.

Huh?

Is heaven enough (was eleven enough)
to ensure that the test of your mettle's not fluff,
some miracle wish for your kettle of fish,
a satirical dish of fine fettle (not kitsch)
to ensure that you'd settle the hash in your cache,
too demure to be nettled to do something rash?

Images of Color

Great Blue in the backyard garden,
regally drawn by what,
reds, yellows, persimmons, pinks,
one lone goldfish white?

No.

He was just pooped
(or pooped)
and flew away,
leaving his regal
behind.

According to Type

When your right hand is just one position off, instead of getting "filled" you get "fukked."

BFFs

How many boffins could a boffin boff
if a boffin could boff boff?

> *Is that too many F an' Bs?*
> *Well then.*

How many boffins could a boffin off
if a boffin could off boff?

> *Better?*
> *No?*
> *Well then.*

Whether or not you boff boff or off,
you will likely boff yourself offin'.

Disney Was Witewawwy Wobbed

What if you make a weawwy bad wefewence
which seems diswespectfuw of Waltew and Elmew?

If you'we vewy vewy cwevew
you bwame Wawnew Bwothews
and ask *them* to say with a weawwy stwaight face:

        "Wailwoad cwossing without any caws;
        can you speww 'it' without any Ws?"

Subtext

There's a cardinal whistling outside my window
singing loud and strong to keep me from noticing
the front pocket where his hand is.

Sounds like church to me.

One Can Never Be Too Little Rich

Once you get some *Cash Smashing Pumpkins*,
Rush to *Chekhov* stuff on your bucket *Liszt*,
always suspicious of young, buff Marlon Brandos yelling, *"Stella!"*
and celiac patients who like hearing *Schütz* after dinner.

Copernican Inversion

Not with a whimper but a bang he came,
too soon for the rest who still thought it best
to sit still in a church whose attention was less
to the light than to windows.

Though Science May with Myths Begin

The world is not flat.
Nothing is certain.
Alice wasn't real.

Part 3

Fig Leaves and Open Arms

The Fig Leaf

Once upon a time,
I did not like the person I was.

Finally,
I threw up that biting apple
from yesterday's Eve
and chose the fig leaf instead.

No Pain, No Gain

Stand naked only
in front of those
who are no match for you.

Hidden Portions

What we love in others
may only be hidden portions
of our own being.

Monkey See

The pleasure of such company
is all we ever seek.

The measure of such love, for me,
is all we ever speak.

We never *do*.

Lust

Lust is no sin of the flesh
but of the mind tainted
by the most off-color
joke.

I Love You Badly

I love you
more than I hate myself.

I can't be all bad.

The Tease

Remember the pain
of wanting what the tease implied
but did not deliver.

Yoo-Hoo, Zarathustra!

Play with me. It's not safe.
That's where the meaning is.

Permutations

Feel the want.
Want to feel the want.
Feel the want to feel the want.
Want to feel the want to feel the want.
Feel the want to feel the want to feel the want.
Want to feel the want to feel the want to feel the want.

One person's "feel to want" is another person's "want to want,"
and so on.

The Loathing

Loathing the shelf on which I sit,
clothing the self I wish to fit
but fear to try,
I become impotent
in the face of possibility.

I am fit to be untied; yet
here I sit with needs denied,
a self all tied in knots untried,
loathing the shelf on which I sit,
clothing the self I wish to fit
but fear to try:
I become impotent
in the face of possibility.

When Alibi Is Love

Not tonight, dear; I have a headache: alibi.
Not tonight, dear; I am writing a song: love.

I Love You, Good-Bye

You loved me to justify your past
when all along
I loved you to justify your future.

Together we killed your past,
and to my surprise
I died with it.

Hypocrisy Unclothed

Whoever said it is better to give than receive
was some dumb celibate priest
who should have had his brains
in his pants.

On Behalf of the Other Half

Be half-human.
It's easier on everyone else.

I've Got Those Ol' Cerebral Blues

One I loved with both halves of the brain.
One I loved with only the right.

Who loses when I plug in both halves?
The one with whom I was lopsided.

The Last Meal

You're sorry you don't love me no more,
and I'm sorry that I still want to make liver and onions
and stand naked in your kitchen.

Mea Culpa

I am not sorry for having loved.
I am sorry for having understood.

Maxima Culpa

We don't celebrate death anniversaries;
we endure them gracefully or should,
unless we dig regret its own grave
and celebrate mea culpa forever after.

The Crush

Someone who had a crush on me
asked what kind of person I liked.

> *He was, of course,*
> *thinking sexually.*

I replied, "Someone smart."

> *So was I.*

Good-Bye, Sadness, Hello

I am sorry I seduced you.
It was what you wanted.
Forgive me.

Not for the Requited

I wish I could ask you to hold me
so I could be that terrified.

Differentiation

Do you know the difference
between a fox and a dog?

About five drinks.

Worthy Applause

"You are addicting," he said,
responding to the thought
of the touch of the hand
that applauds every part
of him.

Remake the Bed

Love, be not proud.
Just change your sheets a little more often.

When the Thrill Is Gone

I once said that if this lasted but one weekend
I would be happy, honored by the experience,
thrilled by the possibility.

Now that it's over,
I don't feel so noble.

The Art House

Form is the house in which art lives.

To the extent that our relationship is art,
it is fair to say that we have been art
without housing.

I mourn, not finding shelter.
I mourn not the art.

The Look of Logic

I only want to see my face
in some eyes wide with wonder.

Logic is like that:
limited.

The Unsettling

Sometimes,
I'd settle for a one-night sit.

Movie Love

Stop asking for the moon,
and give me one of those damn cigarettes.

Looking for Good Bars

So, what am I looking for in a lover?
Something between Mary Poppins and Jaws.

Out in Public

When your eye is open, we make love.
When your "I" is closed, we go out in public.

Titillation

I am tired of being titillated down to my soul.
I'd prefer the experience more locally centered.

Syntactical Imprecision

Knowing what love is is
knowing what love isn't; isn't
that too many verbs?

Part 4

Partisan Lips, No Tongue

The First Compromise

The first compromise
is the last and only test.

Flat Earth

I am so tired of understanding.
Perhaps the Flat Earth Society has a point.

The Man

Dear Santa,

Since last you rode by,
the Man got me
by the throat.

I saw your face.

The Con Game

You're such a fool to disbelieve the facts
and believe the acting.

As California Goes ...

I should be an amendment to the Constitution.

> *What would you say if you were?*

(pause)

No.

I could never be an amendment to the Constitution.
California would fall in the ocean.

> *No.*

> *They'd be the only ones to go along with it.*

For Members Only

The Old Neighborhood Italian American Club
smack-dab in the middle of Chinatown
has a sign on the door that reads "Members Only"
and a sign in the window that reads "God Bless America."

What If He Loses?

Ignore the elephant, heed the jackass,
and pray it isn't a "tortoise and hare" sort of thing.

If...

If Ayn Rand were alive today,
she would disallow using her words
in service of jingoist impulses.

If Ayn Rand were alive today,
she would lead her life simply,
profoundly.

She would, however, tweet:
"Out of despair, life begins."

The Unsaid

While watching *Judge Judy* on TV last night,
I raised my hand to pick my nose
and took an oath
to tell the truth,
the whole truth,
and nothing but the truth,
so help me God.

Does that mean I'm a Republican?

By Any Other Name

The liberal is the new homosexual,
damned faggot type.
Who does s/he think s/he is,
messing with Mother Nature,
genes notwithstanding,
referently confused,
hard to read,
able to serve so openly
in the military?

Praxis

Practice love of the righteous and foolish and wise.
Practice not fearing for your enemy's demise.
Practice not being God.

The New Satan

On the playground of politics
faith has become the new bully.

The Right Answer

When there is no chance for reasoned rebuttal,
the fallow posture and cluck and finger the point to death,
all the while holding their breath and counting to ten
to ponder the depths to which they will sink to cry, "Fowl."

Oh.

That's way too high a number and
they can't spell.

Sorry.

Syntactical Precision

Don't tread on me.
I do gerunds.

If It Walks Like a Duck

God created man in his image.
A man said that.

Woman must cleave to her husband.
A man said that, too.

Duh.

Hidden Persuaders

Sound bites;
subliminal ads using language, not color;
wryly manipulated phrases, not facts;
intentions designed to peak feelings, not pith:

> Blue State, Red State, Left Wing, Right Wing,
> Socialist, Communist, Entitlements, Rights,
> 2nd Amendment as Tea Party Remedy
> and the big mama of non-pithiness:

> *American Exceptionalism!*

Symbol Crashes

Closets, white hoods, Citizens United,
catacombs, confessionals, yellow stars,
crosses bent at right angles, emboldened
like dogma and torture and poison and tea.

Slippery Slope

Bootstraps and silver spoons, once enemies,
now ride in the same Porsche pickup.

Obiter Dicta

It is depressing to see hate so freely offered as reliable data.
Revisionist history is evil no matter who applies it.
Modern politics is fastly becoming an adverb.
Native Americans are not white.
We all squat behind two shoes.
There is no truth.
Higgs boson.

Boycotting Chicken

If cuisine isn't served to your satisfaction,
don't sit down with menu-hate.

Show Me Your Papers

He will probably have a very red neck
and a big red truck with a shotgun rack
when he shoots me.

The Art of Political Persuasion

Pretending to like tea is like
pretending to like Ewe people,
philanthropic gestures,
each a lie.

Victim Abuse

Talk about users, yes indeedy,
but talk about those among the needy
actually bent out of shape and greedy,
not about whether or not they're all seedy
in using the help that is offered them.

(I think I am 47 percent right about this.)

Be Honest at Least

The English said:
>"Upon this rock thou shalt live
>all the days of your lives,
>and we want your crops, your trees,
>and the air you breathe."

The Spanish said:
>"Help us build a church for our God,
>a home we can all pray together in."

Spin

Seeds and lies and loopholes (folly) do amuck the run
by golly Hester, sister Sue, and Polly with another dame
(that Dolly) coddle, toddle, waddle, volley, tricks
and koans to twaddle jolly sticks and stones, to model
squally seeds and lies and loopholes run amuck.

Numbers You Can Wrap Your Mind Around, Not Heart

Reading 20 + 6 = 26, 16 x 6 = 96, 4 x 7 = 28, 27 x 1 = 27, 29 x 1 = 29, 30 x 1 = 30, 47 x 1 = 47, 52 x 1 = 52, 56 x 1 = 56, 124 + 241 = 365, 124 ÷ 20 = 6.2, 241 ÷ 6 = 40.2, 40.2 + 6.2 = 46.4, and 46.4 ÷ 2 = 23.2

is not at all like reading Alison, Ana, Avielle, Benjamin, Caroline, Catherine, Charlotte, Dylan, Emilie, Jack, James, Jesse, Jessica, Madeleine, Noah, Olivia, Chase, Daniel, Grace, Josephine, Victoria, Rachel, Lauren, Dawn, Anne, and Mary.

The former takes only average skill; the latter, incalculable …

> like trying to make sense of Helen or Paris,
> like trying to make sense of Bonnie or Clyde,
> like trying to make sense of metaphysics,
> like trying to make sense of the Erlking's breath.

NRA

I don't understand this passion for guns.

Perhaps it is about paper and game.
Perhaps it is about stick 'em and up.

Either way, there is but one hitch:
coroners never report that a victim died of a personshot.

Civil Is as Civil Does

If you believe in civil rights,
you'll likely believe in taxes and laws,
in metal detectors and gender flaws.

If you don't?

You'll likely surround yourself with yourself
and carry a flag with a snake on it,
or a hood.

The Reproductive Right

When men don't get it, they whine about rights,
especially their right to bare arms and things.

They won't have to worry about courting aborting
until women in Congress begin the extorting
to cut off their balls 'cause they asked for it.

An American Litany

A Latina Supreme Court Justice
administered the Vice-Presidential Oath of Office
to a white guy.

Heaven help us.

A white Supreme Court Justice
administered the Presidential Oath of Office
to a black guy.

Heaven help us.

Oh, I forgot.
The President speaks Spanish.

Heaven help us.

Pro-Life Governor

This is what he said:

> *Isomorphism between countably infinite structures*
> *(satisfying specified conditions, of course)*
> *indicates that any two infinite but countable structures*
> *are isomorphically bound to one set of rules.*
>
> *Increasing the bijection that exists*
> *between the rational and the irrational*
> *will mete Boolean conditions.*

This is what he meant:

> *I'm not anything like you, but trust me.*

Armed Security, English at Ten

Attention all teachers who suck:
arm yourselves!

First Clues

When ceilings part
When boughs break
When pigs fly

When Rosa sat
When Jesus wept
When Junior bought a Rolex

Like Dot Liked Them Slippers

What do you do when the world is all colored
and you want all things pure and pristine,
click them heels together?

No.

You legislate like there was no yesterday.

A Support Group for Facts

By poll are we driven
to a hell of our own making.

Transfusing Stein for Righties

Oh to be so negative, bloodred rose
from a bed of deceit and malice, to beg,
hands in pockets, cat on tongue, dispersions cast,
hell-bent for harried truth.

Fracking for Truth

Throwing your tongue around wrapping your mind around inexactly,
like searching for the right stuff in the wrong way for the right reasons,
may mean that you're inexactly right about reasons and stuff,
exactly wrong about ways.

Lemming Rules

Look out for fifes,
drum majors, banging drums.

Look out for trendy verse,
rushing fools, fearing angels.

Look out for circus barks,
ready marks, readier johns.

Look out for big boots.

Indigenous Lies

Manifest Destiny,
iambic reversal:
first a club, then a hammock.

Bullet Point for the NRA

- Look in the mirror and say this aloud:
  the right to shoot oodles and stacks in seconds' time
  trumps any number of dead babies.

Music, Politics, and Used Cars

Pitch is a bitch.
No one wants to meter.

They May as Well Sing Opera

Like jabberwocky aping cogent thought,
like eunuchs behaving as if they still had some,
they voted no.

Jingo Blue

If the equal distribution of money is a bad thing,
and the unequal distribution of value is a good thing,
then the first is very red for you; the second, very white.

Maxim Two

Toleration without respect
leads to fascism, holocausts,
and xenophobic pricks
who say that size doesn't matter
just before they schedule auditions.

Maxim Three

Beware those who would rather us not see
than not.

Pipe Dreams

Screw sports.
Keep people healthy.
Pass the bong.

Tolerance

I like bald eagles, am suspicious of beasts.
I like shamans and imams and heretics, not priests.

I like Judge Judy, am suspicious of FOX.
I like gay people, women, grandchildren, not jocks.

We Need More Toes and Fingers

Like statistics justifying profit from risk,
like short-term benefits from killing the planet,
like counting the bullets having babies for lunch,
we talk about death in numbers.

Death doesn't kill people,
numbers do.

The New Verb

Trying to grok being second-amendmented
is rather like waiting for Godot by yourself.

The Acquittal

The scene was played out on national TV:
two scripts, one resolution,
plenty of angst.

What's next, *Saturday in the Park with George?*

When Wishes Were Children

Look over there, a bronze female standing tall,
a torch of freedom, hope, promise,
poetry too.

Look over there, huddling:
the hopeful.

Look over there, cowering:
snipers.

Rape

Oh Africa, my Africa,
your land was flat, your horizon was flat,
your sky unscraped by vertical defiance,
mountains of steel.

Your animals, your trees, even birds
know this:

>   periphery was lost
>   when men from the north came looking up,
>   digging tunnels in the sky.

Hangman

The freedom to be has always been lynched
by those for whom trees are gavels.

Cock, Tail, or Tea Party

Hissy fit, hissy fit, what do you mean,
all puffed up and righteous, all shuck, jive, and preen?

Stop acting the cuckolds like randy old queens,
pretending to man-up as if that were keen.

If your prissy is pissy, however it's meant,
be aware that we'll know you're all really quite bent.

Manifest Destiny

What if the Tea Party was indigenous?

You figure it out.
I have my reservations.

The Center

wishing the Left was a little less giant,
wishing each Santa a little less girth,

wishing the Right was a bit less defiant,
wishing like hell they weren't warming the earth.

Snarkasm

God made Blacks, Mexicans, and Gays.
You seem to think He made "Whites" better.
I guess that means He must still need some practice.

Melting the Pot

Having illusions of grandeur?
Think you know what inclusion is?
See if you can pronounce more than five of these:

> priority,
> prioridad,
> priorité,
> priorità,
> vorrang,
> προτεραιότητα,
> приоритет,
> **优先**,
> .ةيولوأ

Danny, Trayvon, Martin, and John

When love suffers a slow death,
the heart breaks little by little,
not all at once.

When love is murdered,
it takes longer.

Part 5

I'm from Missouri

You Can Have It Both Ways[1]

... circumstances change
  and favor the return
  or exit
  of possibility's face ...

---

[1]   Like the Crab Canon in music, this poem is designed to be read both ways to vary the meaning and experience.

The Least Likely Gesture

The trick when you're

                down

                        one

                              day

is to

                            <u>next</u>!

                      <u>the</u>

              <u>up</u>

Line Dancing

Line can
>> destroy the music,
>> remember the ear,

>> changethepaceoftheread,
>> slow
>>> the

>>>> progress

>>>>>>> of

>>>>>>>>>> context,

make images *pop*,
make images

>>>>>>>>>>>>>> (lonely).

Black Hole

·

Under the Table

passing out
the tea he brings to the table
like some dumb drunk too wasted to have tasted
the tea he brings to the table
passing out.

Needs Work

noituLOVE

Now I Get Evelyn Wood

.gip tsilatipac
,ruoh eth yb segrahc ehs eciton ton ll'uoy
gnimmiks dna gninnacs yb gnipoh dna gnipoh
,dooW nylevE dias ",yenom si emiT"

Crescendo e Accelerando[2]

in bed	hungry	parched
mama gone	secrets	(*shhhhhh*)
squeek pinch oops	giggle	kiss
kiss kiss	kiss kiss kiss	kiss kiss kiss kiss
‖:kiss kiss kiss kiss:‖	‖:kisskisskisskiss:‖	(*vamp*)
bite oops	(no giggle)	(*shhhhhh*)

---

2   This poem resulted from a classic problem-solving exercise; i.e., a task defined with limitations and the variables specified. In this case, the task was to write a poem about a physical encounter. The following was specified:
- Limitations: no names, no punctuation, only phrases, G-rated.
- Variables: choice of setting, length, form, inference, tone, etc.

The solution: the writer chose to solve the problem by writing a conceptual poem that looks like it sounds; i.e., the rhythms and silences of both aural and silent readings are intended to be influenced by how and where words, phrases, and symbols are placed on the page.

Part 6

[sic]

Footnote Hell

UTC[3] and BCE[4] were PG[5] and got hitched.
The couple (SIC)[6] was initially aggravated,
thinking the whole ACRONYMS[7] MO[8] a BIT[9] too MUCH.[10]

UTC wanted to make sense of it all,
googling for help with the PC[11] on the QT.[12]

Knowing this, BCE was afraid of the possible OOPS,[13] see,
and purposefully dropped the KID[14] on its head
saving UTC from having to tell the DODO[15] online
(who probably couldn't help MUCH anyway)
she was an acrimonious acronymous BITCH.[16]

Being a BITCH herself, BCE suggested to UTC
that the dropped KID was NSS.[17] UTC agreed![18]

---

[3] UTC stands for **U**niversal **T**ime **C**oordinate, the fancy newish name for **G**reenwich **M**ean **T**ime (GMT). **US C**entral **T**ime is officially UTC-06 as we are six hours behind GMT. Except now that we have **D**aylight **S**avings **T**ime in effect, it's only five hours, but that doesn't change our time zone; we're now UTC-06/DST. UTC takes into account the addition or omission of leap seconds each year by atomic clocks in order to compensate for changes in the rotation of the Earth.

[4] BCE stands for **B**efore the **C**ommon **E**ra; i.e., before the birth of Christ (BC). CE stands for **C**ommon **E**ra; i.e., after the birth of Christ (AD).

[5] **P**rofoundly **G**ifted

[6] SIC is inserted in parentheses after a word or phrase to indicate that an odd or questionable reading of that word or phrase was intended, especially if the preceding word or phrase contains an error or an unconventional spelling. In this case, one might be tempted to read "couple" as a verb form or, more likely, will recognize that SIC also stands for **S**elf-**I**nteraction **C**orrection.

[7] **A C**razy **R**oundup **of N**onsense **Y**ou **M**ust **S**ee

[8] **A M**ethod of **O**perating, a manner of working

[9] **B**asic **I**ntegrated **T**est

[10] **M**any **U**sing and **C**reating **H**ypertext (a collaborative hypertext system)

[11] **P**olitically **C**orrect

[12] **Q**uiet **T**ime

[13] **O**utrageously, **O**ffensively and **P**rofoundly **S**tupid

[14] **K**eyboard **I**nput **D**evice

[15] **D**irector **O**f **D**igital **O**perations

[16] **B**abe **I**n **T**otal **C**ontrol of **H**erself

[17] **N**ot **S**tatistically **S**ignificant

[18] No shit, Sherlock.

Misplaced

I am a [*sic*] man.